BEN CARSON

Books in the Today's Heroes Series

TODAY'S HEROES
BEN CARSON

by Ben Carson
with Cecil Murphey
and Nathan Aaseng

ZondervanPublishingHouse
Grand Rapids, Michigan

A Division of HarperCollins*Publishers*

This book is dedicated to my mother,
Sonya Carson, who basically sacrificed
her life to make certain that my brother
and I got a head start.

Ben Carson
Abridged from the book *Gifted Hands*
Gifted Hands copyright © 1990 by Review and Herald Publishing Association
Abridgment copyright © 1992 by Zondervan Publishing House

Requests for information should be addressed to:
Zondervan Publishing House
Grand Rapids, Michigan 49530

Library of Congress Cataloging-in-Publication Data

Carson, Ben.
    Ben Carson / by Ben Carson with Cecil Murphey.
        p. cm. — (Today's heroes series)
        Summary: The chief of pediatric neurosurgery at Johns Hopkins
University Hospital tells about his life and some of his notable cases.
        ISBN 0-310-58641-0 (pbk.)
        1. Carson, Ben—Juvenile literature. 2. Afro-American neurosurgeons—
Biography—Juvenile literature. [1. Carson, Ben. 2. Physicians. 3. Neurosur-
geons. 4. Afro-Americans—Biography.] I. Murphey, Cecil B. II. Title. III. Series.
    KD592.9.C37A3   1992
    617.4'8'092—dc20
    [B]   92–15925
                                                                                                    CIP
                                                                                                    AC

Abridged by Nathan Aaseng
Edited by Bruce and Becky Durost Fish
Interior designed by Rachel Hostetter
Interior illustrations by Gloria Oostema
Cover designed by Mark Veldheer
Cover illustration by Patrick Kelley

Printed in the United States of America

98 99 00 01 02 / LP / 13 12 11 10

CONTENTS

Chronology of Events

1951. Ben Carson born in Detroit, Michigan, to Sonya and Robert Carson.

1959. Ben's parents divorce, and he is baptized.

1962. Ben begins to read and his grades improve.

1965. Ben tries to stab his friend.

1968. Ben graduates from high school and begins studies at Yale University.

1973. After graduation from Yale, Ben enters medical school at the University of Michigan.

1975. Ben marries Candy Rustin.

1978–82. Ben does his residency at Johns Hopkins.

1983. Ben and Candy move to Australia; their first son, Murray, is born.

1984. Ben becomes chief pediatric neurosurgeon at Johns Hopkins.

1985. Ben performs a successful hemispherectomy on Maranda Francisco.

1987. Ben separates the Binder twins, who had been joined at the back of the head.

1

The Class Dummy

From the time I was eight years old, I knew what I wanted to be when I grew up. I imagined myself traveling to primitive villages around the world. I dreamed of curing the sick, just like those missionary doctors I heard about in church.

Unfortunately only top students get into medical school. I was the worst student in the whole fifth grade at Higgins Elementary School. No one else came close. I didn't understand a thing that was going on in my classes.

If any of my fifth grade classmates or their parents had heard me talking about becoming a doctor, they would have laughed until their ribs hurt. Their teasing was bad enough. After every test we took, their cruel remarks came zinging at me like poisoned darts:

"I know what Ben Carson got! A big zero!"

"Hey, dummy, think you'll get one right this time?"

"Carson got one right last time. You know why? Sheer accident! He was trying to put down the wrong answer, but he goofed."

Sitting stiffly at my desk, I acted as if I did not hear the other students. Sometimes I just smiled back at them. But their words hurt. *I'm just dumb,* I thought, *and everybody knows it.*

How could they help but know it when our teacher, Mrs. Williamson, had us correct each other's math quizzes? After she read the answers, each test was marked and returned to its owner. Then we had to report our score out loud when the teacher called our names.

One day I passed my quiz to the girl behind me. She was the ringleader of the kids who teased me about being dumb. My heart sank when she returned my corrected paper and I saw the score. As Mrs. Williamson started calling the names, I ducked my head in shame. I cringed at the sound of my own name.

"Benjamin?" Mrs. Williamson waited for me to report my score.

I mumbled my reply.

"Nine!" Mrs. Williamson was so pleased she

dropped her pen. She smiled at me. "Why, Benjamin, that's wonderful!" For me to get nine out of thirty math problems would have been more than wonderful—it would have been a miracle!

Before I realized what was happening, the girl behind me yelled, "Not nine! He got none. He didn't get any of them right." Her snickers were echoed by laughs and giggles all over the room.

"That's enough!" the teacher said sharply, but it was too late. I don't think I have ever again felt so lonely or so stupid. It was bad enough that I usually missed almost every question on the tests. But when the whole class laughed at my stupidity, I wanted to drop through the floor.

I was one of the few black kids at our school. Although no one in my white class said anything about my being black, my failure helped convince me that black kids were not as smart as white ones. As the weeks passed, I accepted that I was at the bottom of the class because that was where I belonged.

I should have realized right then that I had no chance of ever becoming a doctor. What were my chances of ever making it through high school, much less going on to medical school? I should have given up my dream and gone on to something sensible.

I probably would have given up if my mother had not been so stubborn. "You weren't born to be a failure, Bennie," she said over and over again. "You can do it! Don't you stop believing that for one second." I used to get mighty tired of hearing those words. There were times when I wished she would realize I was a dumb kid and just let me be. But Mother refused to give in.

Who could have believed that the worst student in Higgins Elementary School fifth grade would one day become a world-famous brain surgeon? That a poor ghetto kid would learn to perform operations too risky for some of the most highly trained surgeons to attempt? That the kid who got zero out of thirty on his math quizzes would regularly snatch the lives of tiny children from the edge of death?

Mother believed. She told me many times, "If you ask the Lord for something and believe he will do it, then it'll happen." My life is living proof that it's true.

2

An Amazing Woman

I could sense that something was not right in my parents' marriage when I was very small. The anger never burst out into the open because my parents did not argue. Instead our house often filled with deathly silence when they were upset with each other. Sometimes I froze with fear or huddled in my room, wondering what was happening when Mommy and Daddy did not talk. My father began to leave the house more and more often.

I loved my father. He was kind and patient and he liked to play with me. He was often away, but when he was home he liked to hold me on his lap.

Ben Carson

He would bring me presents and take me for drives in the car. Many afternoons I'd pester my mother or watch the clock until I knew it was time for my dad to come home from work. Then I'd rush outside to wait for him. When I saw him I'd yell, "Daddy! Daddy!" and rush to meet him. He would scoop me into his arms and carry me into the house.

So I was stunned when Mother sat me down one day and said, "Your daddy isn't going to live with us anymore."

"Why not?" I asked, choking back the tears. "I love my dad. I don't want him to go. Did I do something to make him want to leave us?"

"Oh, no, Bennie. Your daddy loves you."

I burst into tears. "Then make him come back."

"I can't. I just can't." Mother's strong arms held me close, trying to comfort me. "Your daddy did—" She paused, groping for the right words. "Bennie, your daddy did some bad things."

I wiped my eyes with the back of my hand. "You can forgive him then. Don't let him go."

Mother tried to make me understand why Daddy was leaving, but her words did not make much sense to an eight-year-old. Even though Mother said that Daddy had done some bad things, I couldn't think of my father as bad. He had always been good to Curtis and me.

I don't know how long I continued crying the

day Daddy left. My heart was broken because Mother said that my father was never coming home again. To my young, hurting heart the future stretched out forever. I could not imagine a life without Daddy. It was the saddest day of my life.

For weeks I pounded my mother with every argument I could think of to get her to make Daddy come home. Every night when I went to bed I prayed, "Dear Lord, help Mother and Dad get back together again." In my heart I knew God would help them make up so we could be a happy family.

But Dad never came home again.

My shattered life was left in the hands of one amazing woman, my mother, Sonya Carson. Mother pulled off a miracle just battling through life on her own. Yet she still found time to help turn a miracle in mine.

Sonya Copeland grew up in Tennessee as one of twenty-four children in her family. She never advanced beyond the third grade in school. Desperate to escape a bleak home situation, she married at the age of thirteen to a twenty-eight-year-old man. That was my father, Robert Carson. In the late 1940s they moved to Detroit, where my father found a job at an automobile factory. I was born in Detroit on September 18, 1951, two years after my brother, Curtis.

Mother had pulled herself up out of a deep hole to build a respectable life. She had tried hard to make a nice home for her family. Then came the divorce, and suddenly she found herself thrown into a deeper hole than ever. This time she had not only herself to pull out, she also had to carry two devastated little boys along with her.

The most obvious change in our lives was that we were poor. Whenever Curtis and I asked for toys or candy as we had done before, we heard the same answer: "We just don't have any money." In the months after Dad left, Curtis and I must have heard that statement a hundred times. I soon learned to tell from the expression on Mother's face how deeply it hurt her to deny us. After awhile I stopped asking for what I knew we could not have anyway.

In a few instances I could see resentment flash across Mother's face. Then she would get very calm and explain to us that Dad loved us but that he would not give her any money to support us. A few times she went to court, trying to get child support from him. Afterward Dad would send money for a month or two—never the full amount. "I can't give you all of it this time," he would say, "but I'll catch up. I promise."

Dad never caught up. After awhile, Mother gave up trying to get any financial help from him. Yet I can hardly think of a time when she spoke against my father. Only much later in life did Curtis and I learn what Dad had done that was so bad. My father had another "wife" and other children whom we knew nothing about.

Mother never complained to us about her situation, and she did not feel sorry for herself. She tried to carry the whole load herself. She went out of her way to protect us from seeing how bad things were or how badly she hurt.

Several months after Daddy left us, Mother announced, "I'm going away for a few days. Going to see some relatives."

"Are we going too?" I asked with interest.

"No, I have to go alone." Her voice was unusually quiet. "Besides, you boys can't miss school."

Before I could object, she told me that we would stay with neighbors. "I've already arranged it for you. You can sleep over there and eat with them until I come back."

Maybe I should have wondered why Mother left, but I didn't. I was so excited about staying in somebody else's house. It meant better food and a lot of fun playing with the neighbor kids.

Little did I know where Mother really went when she "visited relatives." When the load became too heavy, she checked herself into a mental institution. The divorce plunged her into a terrible period of confusion and depression. Her inner strength helped her realize she needed professional help and gave her the courage to get it.

Ben Carson

Her treatment at the mental hospital provided neighbors with a hot topic of gossip. They also whispered behind her back about the divorce. Because she never talked about the details of her divorce, people assumed the worst and spread wild stories about her.

"I just decided that I had to go about my own business," Mother once told me, "and ignore what people said." She did, but it could not have been easy. People began to avoid her. When she needed them most—while she was struggling to provide a home and earn a living to support us—most of Mother's friends disappeared. She was desperately trying to hang on to her sanity and had no idea what would happen to her kids if she did not stay healthy.

Somehow with all of this going on, Mother managed to bring a sense of security to our family. No matter how bad things were, Mom would comfort me, saying, "Bennie, we're going to be fine." Those weren't empty words either, for she believed them. And because she believed them, Curtis and I believed them too. While I missed Dad for a long time, I felt secure being with my mother and brother because we really did have a happy family. As I grew wiser, I realized that the three of us were actually happier than we had been with Dad in the house. We had peace.

3

Eight Years Old

When my mother had been in the hospital to deliver me, a woman named Mary Thomas had visited her. She was a member of the Seventh-day Adventist church, and she had started talking about Jesus Christ. Mother had listened politely but with little interest. She had heard a lot about God ever since she was a girl in Tennessee. This was nothing new.

Eight years later, Mother checked into the mental hospital following her divorce. She felt all alone in the world. But then Mary Thomas showed up again at her hospital bed. This quiet woman did not try to force anything on Mom or tell her how sinful she was. She simply expressed her own

Ben Carson

beliefs and paused occasionally to read verses from the Bible.

More important than her teaching was the fact that Mary cared about Mother. And right then, Mother needed someone to care. "There is another source of strength, Sonya," Mary said. "And this source can be yours."

Those were exactly the words Mother needed to get back on her feet. She finally understood that she was not alone in the world. With Mary's help, Mother started to study the Bible, even though she could barely read. She would sound out the words. Sometimes she still would not understand the words, but she was not one to give up. She kept at it until she was able to read some of the more difficult passages.

From the time of her conversion, Mother started taking Curtis and me to the Seventh-day Adventist church on Burns Avenue. One Saturday morning, Pastor Ford told a story that set me on the path I would follow the rest of my life. He told of a missionary doctor and his wife who were being chased by robbers in a far-off country. They dodged around trees and rocks, just ahead of the lunging bandits. At last, gasping with exhaustion, the couple reached the edge of a cliff. They were trapped.

Suddenly they saw a small fissure in the rock—an opening just big enough for them to crawl into and hide. When the bandits reached the edge of the cliff seconds later, they could not find the couple. Their victims had just vanished. After screaming and cursing, the bandits finally left.

"The couple were hidden in the cleft of the rock," said Pastor Ford, "and God protected them from harm." He looked out over the congregation. "If we place our faith in the Lord, we'll always be safe."

As I listened, my heart still racing at the thought of the couple's narrow escape, I pictured how wonderfully God had taken care of them. It was the first time in my life that I recognized how much I needed God's help. I thought, *That's exactly what I should do—get sheltered in the cleft of the rock.*

Following the custom of our church, when Pastor Ford asked if anyone wanted to turn to Jesus Christ, I went up to the front of the church. So did Curtis. A few weeks later we were both baptized. The day that I went to the front of the church was the day I decided to set my sights on becoming a doctor, a missionary doctor. I wanted to make people well and help them lead happy lives.

"I want to be a doctor," I said to my mother as we walked home. "Can I be a doctor, Mother?"

"Bennie," she said, "listen to me." We stopped walking and Mother stared into my eyes. "If you ask the Lord for something and believe he will do it, then it'll happen."

"I believe I can be a doctor."

Ben Carson

"Then, Bennie, you will be a doctor," she said. After that, I never doubted what I wanted to do with my life.

But while Mother encouraged me to think toward the future, she had all she could do to survive the present. After a few months of scraping by, Mother realized there was no way to keep up with the house expenses. The only thing she could do was rent out the house, pack us up, and move in with relatives. Dad showed up to help drive us to Boston where Mother's oldest sister lived. Aunt Jean and Uncle William Avery no longer had children at home and were willing to take us in.

Nothing in Detroit had prepared us for life in the low-income apartments in Boston.

"Rats!" I yelled. "Hey, Curt, looky there! I saw rats!" I pointed in horror to a large weedy area behind our building. "And they're bigger than cats!"

"Not quite," Curtis said. "But they sure are mean-looking."

Mostly the hordes of rats lived outside in the weeds or piles of trash. But sometimes they scurried into the basement of our building, especially in cold weather. Once a big snake got into our basement before someone killed it. I would never go down into that basement unless Curtis or Uncle William was with me. My classmates loved to tell stories about neighbors who were killed by snakes.

The stories were not true, but I could not help keeping a frightened eye out for any snakes or rats.

Our apartment was crawling with roaches. The neighborhood was full of broken glass and litter and rotting buildings. Drunks flopped around in the alleys, and squad cars raced up and down the streets.

The Averys provided a lot of love in this bleak setting, especially when Mother continued to check into psychiatric hospitals for treatment. In 1959, they helped put together the most spectacular Christmas of my life. Trying to make up for the loss of our father, Aunt Jean and Uncle William joined Mother in swamping us with toys.

My favorite gift of all time was the chemistry set I got for Christmas that year. I spent hours in the bedroom, studying the directions and working one experiment after another. I mixed chemicals into strange potions and watched in fascination when they fizzled, foamed, or turned different colors. When my experiments filled the apartment with the smell of rotten eggs or worse, I'd laugh until my sides ached.

But mostly, it was Mother who kept us from getting too upset over our new situation. She did not have much free time. With only a third-grade education, she had no chance to find a decent-paying job. She had to work long hours doing housework or caring for children of wealthy people. But she always had a smile for us. What little free time she had, she showered on us. Mother provided such a sense of security that I never worried much about our run-down surroundings. Within a few weeks it felt like a perfectly normal home.

4

School—
Moving Up

You look tired," I said one evening when Mother trudged into our narrow apartment. It was already dark, and she had put in a long day working two jobs.

"Guess I am," she said as she collapsed into the overstuffed chair and kicked off her shoes. With a smile she asked, "What did you learn in school today?"

No matter how tired she was, if we were still up when she got home, Mother asked about school. I got the idea pretty early in life that school was important to her.

Ben Carson

She was satisfied with my schoolwork in Boston. I got good grades at the small, private church school Curtis and I attended. Mother thought that place would give us a better education than the public schools.

But when we moved back to Detroit in 1961, I found out that we had been mistaken. The fifth graders at Higgins Elementary School knew so much more than I that they left me in the dust in every subject. There was no doubt in anyone's mind that I was the dumbest kid in the whole class. I felt stupid from the top of my head to the bottom of my sneakers.

I thought I was too stupid to even read the letters in an eye test that we took halfway through the year. The boy in front of me rattled off every single letter on the examination chart. I squinted, tried to focus, and just barely made out the first line.

But there the problem was not with my brain; it was my eyes. I had no idea that my eyesight had been so bad. The school provided me with free glasses, and when I wore them to school, I was amazed. I could actually see the writing on the chalkboard from the back of the classroom! Getting glasses started me on my climb upward from the bottom of the class.

When my next report card came out, I was thrilled to see that I had gained a D in math. "Benjamin, on the whole you're doing so much better," Mrs. Williamson said to me. *I'm improving, I thought. There's hope for me. I'm not the dumbest kid in the school.*

Despite my excitement and sense of hope, though, my mother was not happy. "Oh, it's an improvement all right," she said. "And I'm proud of you for getting a better grade. But you can't settle for just barely passing. You're too smart to do that. You can make the top math grade in the class."

"But Mother, I didn't fail," I moaned. "I'm doing the best I can."

"But you can do still better, and I'm going to help you." Her eyes sparkled. I should have known from that look that she had already started hatching a plan.

Mother was a goal-setter by nature. That was why we had moved back to Detroit in the first place. Mother had her heart set on getting back into our old house, which she was still renting out. For the time being we lived in a top-floor apartment in a smoggy industrial area while she worked two and three jobs at a time. But as the weeks and months passed, she said, "Boys, just wait. We're going back to our house on Deacon Street. We may not be able to afford living in it now, but we'll make it."

Mother set up the same kind of high goals for Curtis and me, and she wouldn't take no for an answer. I remember when Curtis came home with a note from his junior high counselor. Curtis had to read some of the words to her, but she understood exactly what the counselor had done. He had placed Curtis in the less challenging classes for those kids who would not be going to college.

Curtis was one of the few black kids in the school. Mother had no doubt that the counselor thought blacks were not capable of doing college work.

"They're not going to treat my boy that way," she declared, staring at the paper Curtis had given her.

"What are you going to do?" I asked in surprise. I never imagined that anyone could argue with a decision made by school authorities.

"I'm going right over there in the morning and get this straightened out," she said. The tone of her voice showed she meant business. That evening, Mother told us what had happened. "I said to that counselor, 'My son Curtis is going to college. I don't want him in any vocational courses.'" Then she put her hand on my brother's head. "Curtis, you are now in the college prep courses."

Mother refused to lower her sights for her boys. At the same time she would not settle for anything less than the best we could give. She certainly was not going to let me be content with a D. "I've got two smart boys," she insisted. "Two mighty smart boys. Now since you've started getting better in math, Bennie, you're going to go on. And here's how you'll do it. First thing you're going to do is memorize your times tables." "My times tables?" I cried. "Do you know how many there are? Why that could take a year!"

She stood up a little taller. "I only went through third grade, and I know them all the way through my twelves."

"But, Mother, I can't—"

"You can do it, Bennie. You just have to set your mind to it. You work on them. Tomorrow when I get home from work we'll review them."

I argued a little more, but I should have known better.

"Besides"—here came her final shot—"you're not to go outside and play after school until you've learned those tables."

I was almost in tears. "Look at all these things!" I cried, pointing to the columns in my math book. "How can anyone learn all of them?" But talking to Mother was like talking to a stone.

I learned the times tables. I just kept repeating them until they fixed themselves in my brain. Mother kept prodding me and went over them with me at night. Within days after learning my times tables, math became so much easier. I'll never forget how I practically shouted my score to Mrs. Williamson after another math quiz. "Twenty-four! I got twenty-four right!" School became much more enjoyable. Nobody laughed or called me dummy anymore.

I thought I was on top of the world, but Mother was far from satisfied. She had proven to me that I could succeed in one thing. The next part of her plan was to keep setting higher goals. I can't say I cared much for this plan.

"I've decided you boys are watching too much television," she said one evening, snapping off the set in the middle of a program.

"We don't watch that much," I protested. I tried to argue that some of the programs were educational and that the smartest kids in the class watched television.

As if she did not hear a word, she said, "From now on, you boys can watch no more than three programs a week." She had also decided what we were going to do with all those hours we had spent on television. "You boys are going to go to the library and check out books. You're going to read at least two books every week. At the end of each week you'll give me a report on what you've read."

I couldn't believe it. Two books? I had never read a book in my life except those they made us read at school. But a day or two later, Curtis and I dragged our feet the seven blocks from home to the public library. We obeyed Mother because we loved her and because we could tell when she meant business. But that did not stop us from grumbling the whole way.

Several of Mother's friends criticized her strictness. I heard one woman ask, "What are you doing to those boys, making them study all the time? They're going to hate you."

"They can hate me," she answered, "but they're going to get a good education just the same."

Of course I never hated her. I did not like the constant pressure, but she made me realize the hard work was for my own good. Almost every day she would say, "Bennie, you can do anything you set yourself to do."

Since I have always loved animals, nature, and science, I chose library books on those subjects. My fifth grade science teacher, Mr. Jaeck, discovered my interest and gave me special projects to do, such as identifying fish or rocks. By the end of the year I could pick up just about any rock along the railroad tracks and tell what it was. After reading fish and water life books, I started checking streams for insects. Mr. Jaeck let me look at water samples under his microscope.

Slowly I began looking forward to my trips to the library. The staff there got to know Curtis and me. They began to offer suggestions on what we might like to read. Soon my interests widened to

include books on adventure and scientific discoveries.

As I continued reading, my vocabulary and spelling improved. Up until the last few weeks of fifth grade, our weekly spelling bees were one of the worst parts of school for me. I usually dropped out on the first word. Mrs. Williamson gave us one final spelling bee that covered every word we were supposed to have learned that year. As everyone expected, Bobby Farmer won the spelling bee. He was clearly the smartest boy in the fifth grade. But to my surprise, the final word he spelled correctly to win the contest was "agriculture."

I can spell that word, I thought with excitement. I had learned it just the day before from my library book. As Bobby sat down, a thrill swept through me. *I'll bet I can spell any other word in the world. I'll bet I could learn to spell better than Bobby.*

Learning to spell better than Bobby Farmer challenged me. I kept reading all through the summer. By the time I began sixth grade, I had learned to spell a lot of words. In the sixth grade, Bobby was still the smartest boy in the class, but I was gaining ground on him. I kept improving until, by the time I entered seventh grade at Wilson Junior High, I was at the top of the class.

The very kids who once teased me about being dumb started coming up to me and asking, "Bennie, how do you solve this problem?" I beamed when I gave them the answer. It was fun to get good grades, to earn people's respect. But by then, making it to the top of the class was not good enough for me. Mother's influence had started to sink in. I did not work hard just to be better than the other kids. I did it because I wanted to be the very best I could be—for me.

Ben Carson

5

Problems

My new attitude and success at school did not mean I had easy sailing through the rest of my school days. When I went to Wilson Junior High, I ran into people who were determined to see that black people did not succeed.

That first happened to me as I ran along the train tracks on the way to school. A group of older boys—all white—came marching toward me, wearing scowls of hatred. One of them carried a big stick.

"Hey, you! Nigger boy!"

I stopped and stared, frightened. The boy with the stick whacked me across the shoulder. I staggered backwards, hardly daring to imagine what could happen next. I was just a skinny little kid, and there was nothing I could do against this gang. My heart pounded in my ears, and sweat poured down my sides. The boys stood in front of me and called me every dirty name they could think of. I looked down at my feet, too scared to answer, too frightened to run.

"You know you nigger kids ain't supposed to be going to Wilson Junior High. If we ever catch you again, we're going to kill you." His pale eyes were cold as death. "You understand that?"

My gaze never left the ground. "Guess so," I muttered.

"I said, 'Do you understand me, nigger boy?'"

Fear choked me. "Yes," I croaked, a little louder.

"Then you get out of here as fast as you can run. And you'd better keep an eye out for us. Next time, we're going to kill you!"

I ran then, as fast as I could. I never slowed down until I reached the schoolyard. I stopped using that route and went another way. I never saw the gang again.

That same year Curtis and I joined a neighborhood football league. Football was the popular sport in our area, so both of us were eager to play. Neither of us was large, but we could outrun everybody else on the field. While leaving the field after one practice, Curtis and I suddenly found ourselves surrounded by a group of white men in their twenties. I recognized the same hatred on their faces that I had seen on the gang by the railroad tracks. I was scared.

Then one man stepped forward. "If you guys come back we're going to throw you into the river," he said. Without another word they turned and walked away from us. As we walked home, I said to

Curtis, "Who wants to play football when your own supporters are against you?"

"I think we can find better things to do with our time," Curtis agreed.

We never said anything to anyone about quitting, but we never went back to practice. Nobody in the neighborhood asked us why.

A third, more shocking episode took place the next year. At the end of each year the teachers handed out certificates to the best student in each grade. I had won the certificate for the seventh grade the same year as Curtis won for the ninth. No one was too surprised when I won the award again in eighth grade.

But one teacher was not happy about it. After handing me the award at an all-school assembly, she looked out over the other students. "I have a few words I want to say right now," she began. To my embarrassment, she then bawled out the white kids because they had allowed me to be number one. "You're not trying hard enough," she told them. She had taught me in several classes and had seemed to like me. But there she was telling everyone that a black person should not be number one in a class where everyone else was white.

I was hurt and angered by these incidents, but I didn't say anything. I didn't start hating whites, either. Whenever I ran up against prejudice in life, I could hear Mother's voice in the back of my head:

"Some people are ignorant and you have to educate them." Mother never said things such as, "White people are just. . . ." She never spoke a word of prejudice and never allowed us to. This uneducated woman was smart enough to teach me that people are people. Because of that, I was able to remind myself that when people said unkind things, they were only individuals speaking for themselves; they did not speak for all whites.

At any rate, there was someone working far harder than any bigots or toughs to ruin my life. Me. My problem was a familiar one for junior high kids. I wanted to be accepted as one of the guys.

When I was in eighth grade, Mother had finally realized her dream of moving back to our old house. We were thrilled to finally be going home, but the move meant I had to change schools. At my new Hunter Junior High, I became a special target of a game called "capping."

"Know what the Indians did with General Custer's worn-out clothes?"

"Tell us."

"They saved them and now our man Carson wears them!"

"Get close enough and you'll believe it. They smell like they're a hundred years old!"

That was capping. Capping is a slang word that means to get the better of another person. The idea was to make a sarcastic remark about someone, with a quick barb to keep it funny. Kids would find a victim and compete to see who could say the funniest and most insulting things.

I was a special target because I was a new kid and I did not wear the right clothes. For the first few weeks I didn't say anything when the guys capped on me. That only encouraged them to go at it even harder. I felt hurt and left out, as if I wasn't good enough for them. Walking home, I'd wonder, *What's wrong with me? Why can't I belong?*

There seemed to be no answer. At Wilson, other kids looked up to me because of my grades. But with the Hunter kids, good grades didn't mean much. It was far more important to wear the right clothes, go to the places where the guys hung out, and play basketball. Most of all, you had to learn to cap on others.

I didn't know how to solve the problem of clothes. I knew that Mother was working hard to keep us off public welfare. By the time I reached ninth grade, she had made so much progress that we received nothing but food stamps from the government. Even so, there was no money for stylish clothes.

Like most people, I hated being an outsider. I desperately wanted to belong, and the only way I could belong was to be like the kids at school. I said to myself, "All right, if you guys want to cap, I'll show you how to cap." The next day I waited for the capping to start. Sure enough, a ninth grader said, "Man that shirt you're wearing has been through World War I, World War II, World War III, and World War IV."

"Yeah, and your mama wore it," I said. Everybody laughed.

The kid stared at me, hardly believing what I'd said. Then he started to laugh, too. He slapped me on the back. "Hey, man, that's okay." Soon I was capping with the best of them. The in-crowd stopped tormenting me. They didn't dare throw any insults my way because they knew I would come up with something better.

That solved one problem, but it didn't get me in with the gang. I knew they were ridiculing my clothes behind my back and making fun of me for being poor. To their thinking, if you were poor, you were no good. Although many of the other kids were not much better off than our family, I was ashamed of being poor.

Sometimes my mother sent me to the store to buy bread or milk with our food stamps. I hated to go for fear that one of my friends would see what I was doing. If someone I knew came up to the checkout counter, I pretended I had forgotten something and ducked down one of the aisles until he left. When I saw no one else standing in line, I rushed forward with the items I had to buy.

By the time I hit tenth grade, the peer pressure

had gotten too much for me. "I can't wear these pants," I would tell Mother. "Everyone will laugh at me."

Her answers were always the same: "Only stupid people laugh at what you wear, Bennie. It's not what you're wearing that makes the difference."

"But, Mother," I would plead. "Everybody I know has better clothes than I do."

"Maybe so. I know a lot of people who dress better than I do, but that doesn't make them better."

Almost every day I begged my mother for the right kind of clothes. It seemed I could hardly think of anything else. I had to have those clothes. I had to be like the in-crowd. I knew Mother was disappointed in me, but I didn't care. Instead of coming home after school and doing my homework, I played basketball. Sometimes I stayed out until ten or eleven o'clock.

"Bennie, can't you see what you're doing to yourself?" Mother sighed. "It's more than just disappointing me. You've worked hard. Don't lose all of that now." She knew that I still had my heart set on becoming a doctor.

"I'll keep on doing all right," I would snap back. "Haven't I been bringing home good grades?"

She couldn't argue with me on that point, but I knew she worried.

After weeks of pleading for new clothes, I finally heard the words I had longed to hear. "I'll try to get

Ben Carson

some of those fancy clothes for you," Mother said. "If that's what it takes to make you happy, you'll have them."

"They'll make me happy," I said. "I know they will."

I was so obsessed with what I wanted that I let Mother go without things she needed in order to buy me leather jackets and Italian shirts. These expensive clothes helped me crack into the in-group. I started hanging out with the popular guys. They invited me to their parties and jam sessions.

My grades dropped. I went from the top of the class to being a C student. That was okay with me, though, because I was one of the guys. I was having more fun than I had ever had in my life.

Yet somehow I just wasn't very happy. No matter what clothes Mother bought for me, they weren't enough. I had to have more. Getting into the in-group only made me more anxious about staying in the in-group. I was so crazy about being accepted that I was straying from everything that was important in my life.

6

Terrible Temper

My desperate urge to be one of the guys turned me down a wrong path, but what nearly finished me off was my temper. I was basically a good kid. It usually took a lot to get me mad. But once I reached the boiling point, I lost all control. My temper had gotten me in trouble a few times over the years. I was once embarrassed by a wrong answer I gave in seventh grade English class. As I walked down the hall to my next class, Jerry caught up to me. He was not one of my close friends, and he seemed to take a special delight in my mistake.

"That sure was a dumb thing to say," he taunted.

I shrugged. "Guess so." I felt bad enough without being reminded.

Ben Carson

"You guess?" Jerry's shrill laugh rose above the din of the crowded hall.

I turned my eyes toward him. "You've said some pretty dumb things too," I said, softly.

"Oh yeah?"

"Yeah. Just last week—" Our words flew back and forth. So far I had stayed calm, while Jerry kept getting louder and louder. Finally I turned to my locker. I didn't need this. I ignored him, hoping he would shut up and go away.

My fingers twirled the combination lock. Then, just as I lifted the lock, Jerry shoved me. I stumbled, and my temper exploded. I didn't even think about the twenty pounds of muscle he had on me. I didn't care about the kids and teachers milling in the hall. And I forgot that I had a lock in my hand.

I swung at him. The lock slammed into Jerry's forehead. He groaned and staggered backward. Dazed, Jerry slowly lifted his hand to his forehead. He felt something sticky flowing from a three-inch gash and carefully lowered his hand in front of his eyes. When he saw the blood, he screamed. My anger cooled immediately. By the time the principal called me into his office I was apologizing up and down. "It was almost an accident. I never would have hit him if I'd remembered the lock in my hand."

I meant it, too. Ever since that day with Pastor Ford, I had tried hard to be a good Christian. I had even asked to be baptized a second time. I was ashamed of myself. Christians were not supposed to lose their temper and split people's heads open. I apologized to Jerry and the incident was closed.

Later that year Mother brought home a new pair of pants for me. I took one look at them and shook my head. "No way, Mother. I'm not going to wear them. They're the wrong kind."

"What do you mean 'wrong kind'?" she demanded. She was tired but her voice was firm. "You need pants. Now just wear these!"

I flung them back at her. "No!" I yelled. "I'm not going to wear these ugly things!"

She folded the pants across the back of a kitchen chair. "I can't take them back. They were on special."

"I don't care." I spun to face her. "I hate them and I wouldn't be caught dead in them."

"I paid good money for these pants."

"They're not what I want."

She took a step forward. "Listen, Bennie. We don't always get what we want out of life."

Anger suddenly flamed through my body. "I will!" I yelled. "Just wait and see. I will. I'll—"

My right arm drew back, my hand swung forward. Curtis saw what was happening and jumped me from behind. He wrestled me away from Mother and pinned my arms to my side.

The fact that I almost hit my mother should

Ben Carson

have made me realize how deadly my temper had grown. But I refused to take it seriously, even when I got into a fight with a kid and broke his nose and glasses with a rock.

I was in the ninth grade when the unthinkable happened. Bob and I were listening to a transistor radio when he reached for the dial. "You call that music?" he scoffed as he flipped the dial to another station.

"It's better than what you like!" I yelled, grabbing for the dial.

"Come on, Carson. You always—"

In that instant, blind anger seized me. I snapped open the camping knife I carried in my back pocket and lunged at my friend. With all the strength I could muster, I thrust the knife toward his belly. The blade struck his big, heavy belt buckle with such force that it snapped and dropped to the ground.

I stared at the broken blade and felt my stomach collapse. *I almost killed him,* I thought. *I almost killed my friend.* If the buckle had not protected him, Bob would have been bleeding on the floor, dying or severely wounded.

Bob did not say anything. He just looked at me in shock and disbelief. "I'm sorry," I muttered, dropping what was left of the knife. I could not look Bob in the eye. Without a word, I turned and ran home.

I raced to the bathroom, locked the door, and sank down on the edge of the tub. No matter how tightly I squeezed my eyes shut, I couldn't escape the image—my hand, the belt buckle, the broken knife. And Bob's face. "I must be crazy," I finally mumbled. "Sane people don't try to kill their friends."

Ben Carson

Two hours passed. I sat there in a daze. I felt sick to my stomach, disgusted with myself, and ashamed. I felt as though I could never face anyone again.

I had dreamed of being a doctor since I was eight years old. "Unless I get rid of this temper," I said aloud, "I'm not going to make it. If Bob had not worn that big buckle, he'd probably be dead, and I'd be on my way to jail or reform school."

As I sat there hating myself, with sweat dripping down into my shirt, an urge came from deep inside me. *Pray.* I knew now that I could not handle my temper alone.

"Lord," I whispered. "You have to take this temper from me. If you don't, I'll never be free from it." Tears streamed between my fingers. "You've promised that if we come to you and ask something in faith, you'll do it. I believe that you can change this in me."

Still swimming in misery, I said, "If you don't do this for me, God, I've got no place else to go."

I ran out to get a Bible and returned to my bathroom cell. I opened it and began to read. One verse really impressed me: "Better a patient man than a warrior, a man who controls his temper than one who takes a city" (Proverbs 16:32, NIV).

As I continued to read, I felt as if the verses had been written just for me. I had come to realize that if people could make me angry, they could control me. Why should I give someone else such power over my life? I realized that I had to take charge of my own life. After a while my hands stopped shaking. The tears stopped. A feeling of lightness flowed over me.

I walked out of the bathroom a changed young man. *My temper will never control me again,* I told myself. *Never again. I'm free.* Ever since that day, since those long hours wrestling with myself and crying to God for help, I have never had a problem with my temper. God heard my deep cries of anguish. From that terrible day when I was fourteen, my faith in God has been an important part of who I am.

With my temper problem cured, it was much easier to take charge of my life and focus on the future. Encouraged by my mother and several fine teachers, I watched my grades zoom upward again. In both the eleventh and twelfth grades, I was back among the A students.

Joining ROTC also helped me get back on the right track. ROTC stands for Reserve Officers' Training Corps. Curtis had joined first and done well. I had been so proud of him in his military uniform with medals and ribbons plastered on his chest. I saw other students who seemed so mature and confident, yet friendly. I wanted to be like them. In the second half of tenth grade, I decided to join Curtis.

ROTC helped get me past my hang-up over clothes. In ROTC we had to wear a uniform three days a week. That meant I had to wear regular clothes only two days a week. I had just enough "right" clothes to get me through those two days without kids talking about me.

I earned a lot of medals and received many promotions in ROTC. More important, though, was the fact that I learned how to accept big challenges. One of the most difficult challenges was handling the fifth-hour ROTC unit at our school. The students were so rowdy that none of the other student-sergeants could handle them.

One day Sergeant Bandy, the United States Army instructor who was head of the ROTC unit at our school, came to me. "Carson, I'm going to put you in charge of this class," he said. "If you can make anything out of them, I'll promote you to second lieutenant." That was exactly the challenge I needed.

I got to know the guys in the class and discovered what really interested them. When I found out that most of them enjoyed fancy drill routines, I offered extra drill practice as a reward for their cooperation. When rewards did not work, I made use of my skill at capping on people. Some of them shaped up rather than have me make them look bad by capping on them.

After I had been working hard with the class for

several weeks, Sergeant Bandy called me into his office. "Carson," he said, "the fifth-hour class is the best unit in the school. You have done a fine job." He gave me the promotion he had promised.

I did so well in ROTC that I became one of only three ROTC colonels in Detroit and marched at the head of a Memorial Day parade. I had dinner with General William Westmoreland and was offered a full scholarship to the United States Military Academy at West Point.

Although I was pleased to be offered such a scholarship, I was not really tempted to go into the army. I knew my direction. I wanted to be a doctor, and I was not going to let anything stand in the way.

Ben Carson

7

Not Such a Hotshot

The offer of a full scholarship to West Point flattered me. I was finally beginning to believe what my mother had been telling me about my abilities all along. I graduated third in my class. I did exceptionally well on my Scholastic Aptitude Test (SAT), a test that colleges use to predict how well high school kids will do in college. In fact, my score was unheard of from a student in the inner city of Detroit. Recruiters from the top colleges in the country swarmed around me with scholarship offers because of my achievements.

Unfortunately I carried it a little too far. I started

to believe that I was one of the smartest, most spectacular people in the world. When Yale University in New Haven, Connecticut, not only accepted me but offered to pay ninety percent of my costs, I was happy but not surprised. Maybe I was even a bit arrogant, thinking about how wonderful I was.

I strode onto the Yale campus in the fall of 1969, looking up at the tall, stately, ivy-covered buildings. I figured I would take the place by storm. And why not? I was incredibly bright.

Within a few days I discovered I was not as bright as I thought. I was sitting at the dining room table with several class members who were talking about their SAT scores. One of them said, "I blew the SAT with a total of just over fifteen hundred."

"That's not too bad," another shrugged. "Not great, but not bad."

"What did you get?" the first student asked him.

"Oh, 1,540 or 1,550. I can't remember my exact math score."

I quickly discovered that all the students were bright, and many of them were extremely gifted. It seemed perfectly natural to all of them to have scores in the upper ninetieth percentile. I kept silent, realizing that I ranked lower than every student sitting around me.

The incident opened my eyes, but I did not let it discourage me. I would show them. I would do

Ben Carson

what I always had done before—throw myself completely into my studies. I would learn quickly and zoom to the top of the class.

But I learned that the class work at Yale was unlike anything I had done at Southwestern High School. I had been a good crammer in high school. I had always gotten good test scores by spending the last few days before exams memorizing like mad. It was a shock to realize that this would not work at Yale. You had to stay on top of your work each day or you would fall hopelessly behind. By the time I learned that lesson, it was already too late. Each day I slipped farther and farther behind, especially in chemistry.

Near the end of the first quarter, I walked around the campus, sick with dread. There was no denying it any longer. I had blown it. I was failing freshman chemistry and failing it badly. I didn't have a clue as to what was going on in class. I was staring straight into the face of a horrible truth. If I failed chemistry, I could not stay in the premed program. I would never become a doctor. The taunting voices from fifth grade ran through my head. "Hey, dummy, did you get any right today?"

Who do I think I am? I asked myself. *Just a dumb black kid from the poor side of Detroit. What am I doing at Yale with all these intelligent, rich kids? I don't belong here.*

I kicked a stone and sent it flying into the grass.

Stop it. You'll only make it worse, I thought. I could hear Mother insist, "Bennie, you can do it! You can do anything you want. I believe in you." Still convinced I had no chance to pass, I finally turned to God. "I need help," I prayed. "Being a doctor is all I've ever wanted to do. I've always felt you wanted me to be a doctor. I've worked hard to get this far. But if I fail chemistry, I'm going to have to find something else to do. Please help me know what else I should do."

Back in my room, I sank down on my bed. It was too late. I had done so badly in chemistry that I had only one tiny hope left. My professor had a rule that if failing students did well on the final exam, that would count for far more than the rest of the semester's work. My only chance of passing chemistry was to do well on that final test.

Who was I kidding? I knew I could not pass that test. I sat there in the darkness, my head in my hands. I could not think of a thing I wanted to do in life other than be a doctor. I begged God, "Either help me understand what kind of work I ought to do, or else perform some kind of miracle and help me pass this exam."

From that moment, I felt at peace. I knew that whatever happened, everything was going to be all right.

It was nearly ten P.M. and I was tired. I shook my head, certain that I could not learn the material by

Ben Carson

morning. "Ben, you have to try," I said aloud. "You have to do everything you can."

I sat down with my chemistry textbook for the next two hours, memorizing anything that I thought would help. By midnight the words on the pages blurred. My mind refused to take any more information. I flopped on the bed and whispered in the darkness, "God, I'm sorry. Please forgive me for failing you and for failing myself."

That night I dreamed that I was sitting in the chemistry lecture hall. The door opened and someone walked into the room and started working out chemistry problems on the board. I took notes of everything he wrote. When I awoke, I could remember the problems. Hurriedly, I wrote them down before they faded from memory.

My steps sounded hollow on the wooden floor as I walked into the lecture hall. I was numb from cramming and from despair. The professor came in and handed out booklets of examination questions to the six hundred students. At last, heart pounding, I opened the booklet and read the first problem. In that moment I thought I had entered a twilight zone or some sort of never-never land. I skimmed through the booklet, laughing silently with joy and disbelief. The exam problems turned out to be identical to those written by the shadowy dream figure in my sleep! There was no time to wonder about what was happening. I was so excited about recognizing the problems that I worked quickly, afraid I'd lose what I remembered. By the end of the test, the questions no longer looked familiar. I didn't get every problem right, but I knew I would pass.

"God, you pulled off a miracle," I said as I left the classroom. "I promise you that I'll never put you in that situation again." Thinking about what had happened, I felt small and humble. Despite my failure, the mighty God of the universe had forgiven me and had come through to pull off something marvelous for me.

When the final chemistry grades came out, Benjamin S. Carson scored ninety-seven—right up there with the top of the class.

After this experience, I had no doubt that I would be a doctor. I had cooled on the idea of being a missionary doctor, but I felt certain that God had special things for me to do. I had to do my part by preparing myself and being ready. When I graduated from Yale in 1973, I was far from the top of my class. But I had worked hard to achieve a good grade point average. I knew I had done my best, and I was satisfied.

8

Asleep at the Wheel

I met Candy when I was a college junior. She was one of many freshmen I met at a reception in suburban Detroit for new Yale students from Michigan. "That's one good-looking girl," I thought when I saw her. She was bubbly, and she wandered all over the place, talking to this one and that. She laughed easily, and during the few minutes that we talked, she made me feel good. I admired her outgoing, friendly personality.

While I was at Yale, friends often said, "Ben, you ought to get together with Candy." Meanwhile, Candy's friends were telling her, "Candy, you and

Ben Carson ought to get together. You just seem right together." I was not interested in love, though. All my concentration was fixed on becoming a doctor. With many hard years of study ahead of me, I figured it would be a long time before I could think about romance. Even if I had been thinking about romance, I was shy and had never done much dating.

I saw Candy at school from time to time since we were both taking many of the same classes. The more I found out about her, the more I admired her. She was a fine student and a talented violinist. I had come to enjoy many kinds of music, so I enjoyed talking about that subject with her. When the church I was attending needed an organist, I told Candy about it. She tried out for the job but ended up singing in the choir with us. Candy wasn't one to talk much about religious things and she had little Bible background. But she found a home at Mt. Zion Church. "The people loved me into faith," she says.

Candy and I became friendly enough with each other that we fell into the habit of meeting each other after class. In spite of wanting to avoid romance, I was beginning to like Candy a lot.

Just before Thanksgiving of my senior year, Yale paid Candy and me to do some recruiting in the Detroit area high schools. We had a wonderful time together, driving about in a little rented Pinto. It was not exactly a successful mission. Our job was to interview students who had combined SATs of at least twelve hundred. We did not find one student in the inner-city schools who reached that score. The only students we interviewed were from some of the wealthier suburbs.

I spent some time introducing Candy to my mother and a few of my old friends. That took longer than I had planned. By the time we headed back for Connecticut, we were pressed for time. We would have to drive straight through the night in order to get the Pinto back to the rental agency by eight o'clock the next morning.

We had done so much interviewing and visiting with friends that I had not had one decent night's sleep since leaving Yale ten days earlier. "I don't know if I can stay awake," I told Candy with a yawn. Most of the driving would be on interstate highways. What could be more boring to my sleep-starved body than watching endless miles of straight road on a dark, moonless night.

By the time we crossed the line into Ohio, Candy had drifted off to sleep. I did not have the heart to awaken her. The busy schedule had been tough on both of us. I figured that she could rest a couple hours and then be ready to take over the driving.

At about one in the morning, I was zooming along Interstate 80 near Youngstown, Ohio. It had been half an hour or more since I had seen another vehicle. I felt relaxed, everything under control. The heater kept us comfortably warm.

I grew so comfortable that I drifted off to sleep. Suddenly the car's vibration jarred me awake. My eyes popped open as the front tires struck the gravel shoulder. The Pinto veered off the road, its headlights streaming into the blackness of a deep

Ben Carson

ravine. I yanked my foot off the gas pedal, grabbed the steering wheel, and fiercely jerked to the left.

In those few seconds, my life flashed before my eyes. *This is it,* I thought. *I'm going to die. This is the end.* Those words kept rumbling through my head.

Turning so abruptly at that high speed, the car should have flipped over. But a strange thing happened. The car went into a crazy spin, around and around like a top. I let go of the steering wheel and braced myself for instant death.

All at once the Pinto spun to a stop in the middle of the lane next to the highway shoulder. It was headed in the right direction, the engine still running. Hardly aware of what I was doing, my shaking hands steered the car onto the shoulder. A heartbeat later, a huge, eighteen-wheel truck roared through the lane in which I had been stopped. Had it arrived seconds earlier, it would have plowed into us. I turned off the engine and sat quietly, trying to breathe normally again. My heart felt as if it were racing at two hundred beats per minute. "I'm alive!" I kept repeating. "Thank you, God. I know you've saved our lives."

Candy was so tired that she slept through the whole experience. But she heard me muttering and opened her eyes. "Why are we parked here?" she asked. "Anything wrong with the car?"

"Nothing's wrong," I said. "Go back to sleep."

"Everything can't be fine if we're not moving. What's going on? Why are we stopped?"

I leaned forward and flipped on the ignition. "Oh, just a quick rest," I said casually, as I pulled back onto the road.

"Ben, please—"

With a mixture of fear and relief, I let the car come to a stop far onto the road shoulder and turned off the key. "Okay," I sighed. "I fell asleep back there. . . ." My heart still pounded as I told her what had happened. "I thought we were going to die," I finished.

After hearing the story, Candy reached across the seat and put her hand in mine. "The Lord spared our lives. He's got plans for us."

"I know."

Neither of us slept the rest of the trip. Later on the drive I told Candy how much I liked her and we shared our first kiss. From then on, Candy and I were together all the time. Our being together did not hurt my studies. With Candy at my side, encouraging me, I became even more determined to work hard. When I moved on to medical school at the University of Michigan, Candy still had two years of schooling at Yale. We wrote to each other every day. One time I called her at Yale, and we got carried away. We lost all track of time and talked for six straight hours. Maybe we were both lonely or having a hard time. Strangely, the six-hour call never came through on my bill. I wonder if the phone company looked at the charges and thought it must have been a mistake. Who could possibly talk for that long?

After what seemed like a lifetime of waiting, Candy graduated from Yale in the spring of 1975. We were married that summer, between my second and third years of medical school.

9

Changing the Rules

Although my medical school instructor was a skilled surgeon, he was having some trouble performing the operation. "This is the hardest part," he said, as he probed the patient with a long, thin needle. "Just finding the foramen ovale." The foramen ovale is the opening at the base of the skull.

As I watched him, I thought, *There ought to be an easier way to find that.* Having to hunt for the foramen ovale wasted precious surgery time. Then I started to argue with myself. *You're new at neurosurgery [surgery involving the nervous system].*

Ben Carson

You think you know everything already? Remember, these guys have been doing this kind of operation for years.

Yeah, answered another inner voice, *but that doesn't mean they know everything.*

Leave it alone, I answered myself. *One day you'll get your chance to change the world.*

I might have stopped arguing with myself except that I loved finding new answers to old problems. In my life I had often enjoyed success by doing things a little different from the normal, by changing the rules.

For example during one summer break from college, I had worked as a supervisor with a highway crew. Our job was to clean up the trash along the highways.

Most of the other highway supervisors had a horrible time with discipline problems. The kids who worked for them could give hundreds of reasons for not putting any effort into their work: "It's too hot to work." "I'm too tired from yesterday." "Why we gotta do all this? Tomorrow people will just litter it all up again." "Why should we kill ourselves at this? The job doesn't pay enough to do that."

Other supervisors figured that if each person in the crew filled a few plastic bags a day, they were doing well. The workers could do that much in less than an hour, and I knew it. It seemed a waste of time to let my six-person crew loaf around picking up a dozen or two bags of litter a day.

The fourth day on the job I said to my guys, "It's going to be real hot today—"

"You can say that again!" they all agreed.

"So, I'm going to make you a deal," I said. "Beginning tomorrow, we start at six in the morning while it's still cool—"

"Man, nobody in the world gets up that early—"

"Just listen to the whole plan," I said. "If we all get on the road at six, all you have to do is fill up 150 bags and you're off for the rest of the day. You still earn a full day's pay. But you have to bring in 150 bags no matter how long it takes."

At six o'clock the next morning, all six of the workers were ready to go. And how they worked! They learned to clean a whole stretch of highway in two to three hours. Most crews would not get that much done in a day.

"Okay, guys," I said as soon as I counted the last bag. "We take the rest of the day off." My crew loved coming back to the department of transportation at nine o'clock, while the other crews were barely into their workdays.

"You guys going to work today?" one of my guys would yell. "Hope you don't get sunburned out there!"

We weren't supposed to do things that way.

Crews were supposed to work a nine-hour shift with an hour off for lunch. Yet not one supervisor ever commented on what I was doing with my crew. They kept quiet because we were doing the job faster and better than any other crew.

I tried to apply the same type of creative thinking to the problem of finding the foramen ovale. After several days of brainstorming and trying different techniques, I hit upon a simple technique. I put a tiny metal ring on the outside surface of the skull behind the area where the foramen ovale should be. I then put another ring on the front of the skull. Then I passed an X-ray beam through the skull and turned the head until the beam passed between both rings. At that point, the foramen falls in between.

The procedure seemed simple and obvious, but apparently no one had thought of it before. I did not bother to tell anyone about it at first. I wasn't concerned with impressing anybody; I just wanted to be able to develop a method that worked for me.

The method worked so well in my surgeries that my professors asked me how I was finding the foramen so quickly. I demonstrated the technique for them. The head professor watched, shook his head slowly, and smiled. "That's fabulous, Carson." I was fortunate in having professors who did not resent a young whippersnapper coming up with an idea they had not thought of.

Actually, I was changing the rules just by being where I was. Black kids from the ghetto were not expected to thrive in medical school. But I completed my courses at the University of Michigan Medical School and then served as an intern and a resident at Johns Hopkins University Hospital in Baltimore, Maryland. Johns Hopkins enjoyed an international reputation for excellence, and I had been one of only two interns accepted in neurosurgery out of about 125 applicants.

My being black caught some people at Johns Hopkins off guard. Once as I was approaching a nurses' station, one of the nurses paused to look at me.

"Yes?" she asked. "Who did you come to pick up?" From the tone of her voice, I knew she thought I was an orderly, an aide who does general tasks around a hospital. "I didn't come to pick up anyone," I said with a smile. "I'm the new intern."

"New intern? But you can't—I mean—I didn't mean to—" the nurse stuttered, trying to apologize.

"That's okay," I said. "I'm new, so why should you know who I am?" The only black people she had seen on the floor had been orderlies. Why should she think anything else?

The first time I went into the intensive care unit, another nurse signaled me. "You're here for Mr. Jordan?"

"No, ma'am, I'm not."

"You sure?" she asked with a frown. "He's the only one who's scheduled for respiratory therapy today."

By then I had come closer, and she could read my badge with the word *intern* under my name.

"Oh, I'm so very sorry," she said. I could tell she was, and so I just smiled and went on. I knew that people act on their past experiences. She had never met a black intern before and so assumed I had to be something else.

There was one doctor at Johns Hopkins who could not seem to accept having a black intern. He never said so to my face, but he was constantly rude and insulting to me. The conflict came into the open one day when I asked, "Why do we have to draw blood from this patient? We still have—"

"Because I said so," he roared.

I did what he told me. Several times that day, he snapped back the same reply to my questions. Late in the afternoon, something happened to upset him and he took out his anger on me. "You really think you're something, don't you? Everybody is always talking about how good you are, but I don't think you're worth the salt on the earth. As a matter of fact, I think you're lousy. I want you to know, Carson, that I could get you kicked out of neurosurgery just like that." He continued to rant for several minutes.

When he finally paused, I asked in my calmest voice, "Are you finished?"

"Yeah!"

"Fine," I answered, and he stopped ranting. I wasn't going to let him make me react and make an issue of it. He never did anything to me, and nobody else ever voiced any complaints about me.

With that one exception, people at Johns Hopkins were very accepting and supportive of me. Once a woman complained to my superior, Dr. Donlan Long, that she did not want a black doctor in on her case.

Dr. Long had a standard answer to that. "There's the door. You're welcome to walk through it. But if you stay here, Dr. Carson will handle your case." No matter how strongly any patients objected, they learned that Dr. Long would dismiss them on the spot if they said anything more. So far as I know, none of the patients ever left!

10

Brain Surgery

Although I had been training for many years to become a doctor, I was thrown into the firing line rather suddenly. When I was a resident at Baltimore City Hospital in 1981, paramedics brought in a patient who had been severely beaten on the head with a baseball bat. This attack took place at a time when most of our surgeons were attending a conference in Boston. One neurosurgeon was left on call to cover all the Baltimore hospitals.

The patient was fading rapidly. I kept trying to call the surgeon on call but could not locate him. As the minutes slipped away, I realized the man would die unless something was done quickly. But I was not supposed to perform surgery without an attend-

ing surgeon present. *What should I do?* I wondered. *I am not very experienced. What if I run
into a problem I can't handle? What if something
goes wrong and I am held to blame for his death?*

The physician's assistant knew what I was
going through. He said just three words to me: "Go
for it."

"You're right," I answered. Hoping I sounded
confident and competent, I said to the head nurse,
"Take the patient to the operating room." By the
time the operation actually began I was perfectly
calm. It was not a simple operation. Part of the
patient's brain was swelling so badly that I had to
remove it. But we had no problems during surgery.
The man woke up a few hours later and recovered
completely.

In 1983, after I completed my training in the
United States, Candy and I went to Australia. I
served there as a senior registrar, which is a special
position they have in Australia for those who are
making the jump from being a resident (final-stage
student) to being a full-fledged doctor.

We had not been there a month when an
extremely difficult case came to my attention. The
senior consultant, my superior, had diagnosed a
young woman as having a large tumor at the base
of her skull. This type of tumor causes deafness
and weakness of the facial muscles. Eventually the
patient becomes paralyzed. The consultant told the

Ben Carson

patient that the tumor could be removed. But he advised her that, unfortunately, he could not take it out without destroying her cranial nerves.

After hearing this, I asked the senior consultant, "Do you mind if I try to do this using a microscopic technique? If it works, I can possibly save the nerves."

"It is worth trying, I'm sure."

While the words were polite enough, I could tell he was really thinking, "Just try it, you young hotshot. You'll fall flat on your face." I knew there was a good chance he was right.

I went ahead with the surgery. I operated on the woman for ten hours. By the time I finished, I was completely exhausted. But it proved to be worth the effort. I had completely removed the tumor without bothering the woman's cranial nerves. The senior consultant told her she would likely enjoy a complete recovery. A short time after her recovery, the woman became pregnant. When the baby was born, she named the child after the consultant because she thought he had done the delicate work. But the others on our staff knew.

After that surgery, the other senior consultants showed me enormous respect. From time to time one of them would come up to me and ask, "Say, Carson, can you cover a surgery for me?"

Eager for experience, I never turned down a case. That gave me a tremendous load. After less than two months in the country, I was doing two, maybe three, craniotomies a day—opening people's heads to remove blood clots and repairing damaged blood vessels.

I did a lot of tough cases, some absolutely spectacular. For instance, the fire chief in the city of Perth had an incredibly large tumor that had grown around a number of major blood vessels. I had to

Ben Carson

operate on the man three times to get all the tumor out. The fire chief had a rocky course, but eventually he did extremely well. In my one year in Australia, I got so much surgical experience that I felt capable and comfortable working on the brain. I often thanked God for the experience and training it provided.

Within months after my return to the United States, the chief of pediatric (children's) neurosurgery at Johns Hopkins resigned. Dr. Long recommended to the hospital board of directors that I be named to take his place. "I am fully confident that Ben Carson can do the job," he told them. No one on the board objected. When I heard the news, I could hardly believe it was true. I had dreamed of becoming a doctor ever since I was eight. Yet with all my confidence, I had never expected to be the chief pediatric neurosurgeon at Johns Hopkins before I reached my thirty-fourth birthday!

Within a year of my appointment at Johns Hopkins, I faced one of the most challenging surgeries of my life. The little girl's name was Maranda Francisco, and I had no way of knowing the influence she would have on my career.

Although born normal, Maranda began having powerful seizures at eighteen months. By her fourth birthday, the seizures concentrated on the right side of her body and became more frequent. By the time I heard about her situation in 1985, Maranda was experiencing up to one hundred seizures a day, as often as three minutes apart.

Because the seizures took up so much of her time and energy, Maranda was forgetting how to walk, talk, hear, and learn. She had to be fed through tubes because of the danger of choking on her food. She needed constant medication and had been on thirty-five different drugs at one time or another.

Maranda's condition was called Rasmussen's encephalitis, an extremely rare brain disease. The Franciscos were told that there was nothing that could be done. But Terry Francisco checked on every lead she could find that might help her daughter. One of these led her to Dr. John Freeman at Johns Hopkins.

"Maranda sounds like she might be a good candidate for a hemispherectomy," Dr. Freeman said. A hemispherectomy is the removal of one side of the brain. Dr. Freeman studied all her records and then asked me what I thought about performing the surgery.

I had recently come across some material about hemispherectomies. The information did not sound encouraging. The operation was so dangerous that few surgeons would even consider it. Many patients either bled to death or suffered serious brain damage. I was not at all convinced a hemispherectomy was a good idea.

"Give me some time to read up on this," I told Dr. Freeman.

After lengthy study of medical articles, I met with Mrs. Francisco. "Yours is the only hospital where we've received any real hope," Mrs. Francisco said. "We've tried so many doctors and hospitals. They end up telling us there's nothing they can do for our daughter. Please, please help us."

I agreed to consider doing the operation. I tested and studied Maranda and did some more research. Finally I told Mrs. Francisco, "I am willing to attempt a hemispherectomy. But I want you to know that I have never done one before. It's a dangerous operation. Maranda may well die in the operating room. If not, she could be paralyzed or have severe brain damage."

Mrs. Francisco's eyes met mine. "And if we don't agree to the surgery, what happens to Maranda?"

"She'll get worse and die."

"If there is a chance for her—even a small chance—yes, please operate."

I met with the Franciscos one last time the night before surgery to make sure they understood the situation. As I got up to leave, I said to the parents, "I have a homework assignment for you. I give this to every patient and family member before surgery."

"We'll do anything," they said.

"Say your prayers. I think that really does help." I was a little anxious as I went home that night. So many things could go wrong with Maranda. But I knew that we were at least giving this pretty little girl a chance. I finally said, "God, if Maranda dies, she dies, but we will know that we have done the best we could for her."

Right from the beginning of the surgery, we had problems. Maranda's brain was swollen and unusually hard. It bled anytime an instrument touched it. We had to keep calling for more blood. Slowly, carefully, hour after hour, I inched away the swollen left half of Maranda's brain. Instead of the expected five hours, we stayed at the operating table for ten hours. All that time, I had to avoid fragile parts of Maranda's brain and ease the brain tissue away from the life-giving veins.

Finally we were finished. As we stepped away from the operating table, our team knew we had successfully removed the damaged half of Maranda's brain. But none of us knew what would happen next. Would the seizures stop? Would Maranda ever walk or talk again? I watched her closely as she awakened in the operating room. She moved a little but did not respond when the nurse called her name. *It's early,* I thought.

I followed as Maranda was wheeled out of surgery. The Franciscos, after spending ten torture-filled hours in the waiting room, ran to meet us.

"Wait!" Mrs. Francisco called softly. Her eyes were red-rimmed, her face pale and gaunt. She bent down and kissed her daughter.

Maranda's eyes fluttered open for a second. "I love you, Mommy and Daddy," she said.

"She talked!" a nurse squealed. "She talked!"

We had hoped for recovery. But none of us had considered that Maranda could be so alert so quickly. We had removed the part of her brain that controls the speech area. Yet she was talking! I stood there, amazed and excited, as I silently shared in that incredible moment. Maranda opened her eyes. She recognized her parents. She was talking, hearing, thinking, responding. Silently I thanked God for restoring life to this beautiful little girl.

The news rippled down the corridor. The whole staff, including ward clerks and aides, ran up to see with their own eyes.

"Unbelievable!"

"Isn't that great!"

I even heard a woman say, "Praise the Lord!"

The surgery was a breakthrough event. Reporters started coming around. Television programs such as *Evening Magazine* and *Donahue* featured the miraculous operation. I did not consider the surgery to be that newsworthy. Recent advancements had made it all but certain that surgeons would begin performing successful hemispherectomies. I was not interested in publicity. It was enough to know that in August 1985, Maranda Francisco got her most desperate wish. Since that time, she has had no more seizures.

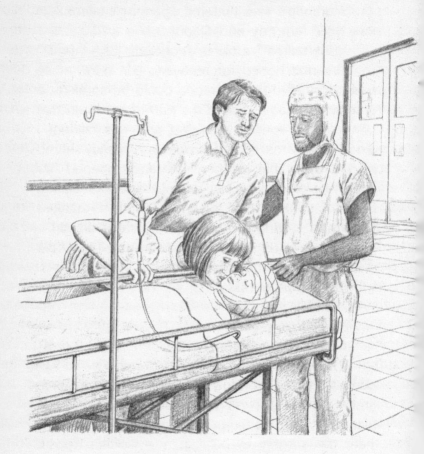

Ben Carson

11

"It's Too Risky"

Beth Usher made no such immediate recovery. She had started having frequent seizures at about age six after falling from a swing in 1985. Her mother happened to read an article about the hemispherectomies we were doing at Johns Hopkins. Immediately Mrs. Usher called us and arranged for an interview. When I met Beth in July 1986, she had actually improved. She was down to as few as ten seizures a week and was bright and vivacious. After listening to my grim report on the dangers of hemispherectomies, the Ushers decided, "She's doing too well. We'd better not risk it."

But after they returned home, Beth began to experience more seizures. When she returned to us three months later, we were alarmed at how much worse she had become. Her speech was slurred, and she was losing the use of part of her body.

The poor Ushers did not know what to do. At least they now had Beth alive, although she was obviously getting worse. "Go home and think about this," I suggested. "Be sure of what you want to do."

Back home, Beth made plans to be in a Christmas play at school. The part meant everything to her and she practiced hard. But during the actual performance, she had a seizure. She was devastated. That day the family decided to go through with the hemispherectomy. The surgery went well with no complications.

Beth remained sluggish after the operation and could hardly be awakened. That reaction disturbed me. I ordered a CT scan that showed her brain stem was swollen. I tried to reassure her parents, "She'll probably get better over the course of a few days once the swelling goes down." But I could see by the worry on their faces that they did not completely trust what I was saying. For hours they stood by her bed in the intensive care unit. They stared at her face and watched the rise and fall of her little chest.

"Beth. Beth, darling," I heard them say over and over.

Finally, weighed down by despair, they left. I felt terrible. All we could do was keep Beth's vital signs steady and wait for her brain to heal. Every day I examined her and checked her records. I tried to reassure the Ushers that Beth would bounce back. Yet I couldn't be positive that Beth would ever wake up. The days passed, and Beth did not improve.

Other doctors and nurses on the staff kept offering encouragement to the Ushers and to me. "It's going to be all right, Ben," they would say. But each day it became harder to walk into the room and face Beth's parents. They looked at me with despair, no longer daring to hope.

One night her dad was lying on a cot in her room, unable to sleep. It was nearly two o'clock in the morning.

"Daddy, my nose itches," came a small voice.

"What?" he cried, jumping out of his cot.

"My nose itches." "Beth talked! Beth talked!" Mr. Usher ran into the hallway, so excited that he didn't realize he was wearing only undershorts. "Her nose itches!" he yelled at the nurse.

Those words were the beginning of Beth's recovery. She continued to improve rapidly. Not only did she return to school, but within a few years she was the top student in her math class.

Each of the hemispherectomies I have done has been a story in itself. Thirteen-year old Denise Baca from New Mexico was in a constant state of seizure when she came to us. Unable to control her breathing because of the constant convulsions, she had to be on a respirator. She was paralyzed on one side and had not spoken for several months.

Medical tests showed that her seizures were occurring in two of the most important sections of her brain. "There is nothing that can be done for her," her parents were told.

A friend, however, alerted Denise to what we were doing at Johns Hopkins. We agreed to evaluate her. Several of my colleagues thought we would be crazy to attempt a hemispherectomy with Denise. This kind of operation was best done on very young patients. Besides, Denise's poor health made her a poor risk to survive any operation, much less one so serious. Finally, the seizures were coming from areas that made surgery dangerous, if not impossible. One critic predicted, "She'll die on the table just from the medical problems, let alone the hemispherectomy."

Those of us most involved in these types of operations at Johns Hopkins thought it was worth a try. But the heated arguments over the issue made us uncomfortable. We did not want to create bad feelings and so we held off for awhile. For days I asked God to help us resolve the problem.

Then the issue took care of itself. Our most outspoken critic left the country for a five-day conference. We decided to take advantage of his absence and do the operation.

I explained the risks to Denise's parents as I did

Ben Carson

to all families facing this choice. "If we don't do anything, she's going to die. If we do something, she may die, but at least we have a chance." The parents agreed to the surgery.

After the operation, Denise remained in a coma for a few days. When she awakened, she had stopped seizing. By the time she was ready to go home, she was starting to talk. Weeks later, Denise returned to school. She has progressed nicely ever since.

That case taught me the importance of sticking to my guns when I really believed in what I was doing, regardless of what critics said. It is a lesson I have had to draw on several times in my career.

Perhaps the farthest I ever went out onto a limb for a patient was the case of Charles in the summer of 1988. Charles was ten years old when he was struck by a car. His condition was so critical that we told the mother he probably could not recover. Within three days Charles was on the brink of death. I sent my senior resident to explain to the mother that I thought we should take Charles to the operating room immediately. We would remove a portion of his brain as a last-ditch effort to save his life. "It may not work," the resident told her, "but Dr. Carson thinks it's worth a try."

"Absolutely not!" the mother cried. She was reeling from shock and grief. "You will not do that to my boy! Just let him die in peace!"

I then went to see Charles's mother. I spent a long time explaining in detail that we were not going to cut the boy in pieces as part of some experiment. My plan was to open up the skull and create some room for the swollen brain to expand and heal. She still hesitated. I told her about a little girl named Bo-Bo, a patient of mine who had survived a similar operation. "Look, I don't know about this surgery," I said. "Maybe it's the smallest glimmer of hope, but we can't just throw it away, can we?"

Once Charles's mother understood exactly what I would do, she asked, "You mean there really is a chance that Charles might live?"

"With surgery, yes. Without it, no chance whatsoever."

This time she permitted the surgery, and we rushed off to the operating room. As expected, Charles remained in a coma afterward. For a week, nothing changed.

It is heartbreaking to watch parents sit by the bedside of a child in a coma. I could not promise a recovery. I could only give hope.

Many others had long since given up hope. More than one staff member said something to me like, "The ball game's over. We're wasting our time."

At one staff meeting that I was not able to

Ben Carson

attend, my actions came in for some heavy criticism.

"I think the operation was a foolish thing to do," said one of the other doctors.

Another agreed. "This patient has not yet recovered, and he's not going to recover. In my opinion, it is inappropriate to attempt this kind of procedure."

Maybe I am just stubborn, but I was not ready to give up. On the eighth day after surgery, a nurse noticed Charles's eyelids fluttering. Soon Charles started to talk. He has made great progress ever since. Although he may experience some seizures, we believe he's going to be fine in the long run. Charles is an active, walking, talking boy with an energetic personality. His mother clearly is thankful to have her son alive. It is another instance when I am glad I did not listen to my critics.

The fact that many of my surgeries are extremely risky means that not every story has a fairy tale ending. A baby, whom I'll call Jennifer, began having terrible seizures within days after her birth. Her poor mother was devastated by it all. We discovered that the problem seemed to be coming from the right side of Jennifer's brain. After studying everything carefully, I decided to take out only the back part of that side of the brain. The surgery seemed successful. The five-month old girl recovered quickly and had far fewer seizures. She started responding to our voices and grew more alert. For a while.

Then the seizures began again. Six months after the first surgery, we were back in the operating room to remove the rest of the right hemisphere. The eight-hour operation went smoothly. Little Jennifer woke up after the operation and started moving her entire body. Shortly after Jennifer's surgery, I left for home, a drive of thirty-five minutes. Two miles before I reached the house, my beeper sounded. Somehow I knew it had something to do with Jennifer. "Oh, no," I groaned, "not that child."

Since I was so close to home, I hurried to the house and called the hospital. The head nurse told me, "Shortly after you left, Jennifer's heart stopped. They're trying to revive her now." I jumped back into my car and made the thirty-five-minute trip in twenty minutes. The team was working on the infant when I arrived. I joined them and we tried everything to get her back. *God, please, please don't let her die,* I pleaded.

After ninety minutes, I turned to the nurse. "She's not coming back," I said. I hurried to the room where her parents waited. Their frightened eyes locked with mine. "I'm sorry—" I said, and that's as far as I got. For the first time in my adult life, I cried in public. I felt so bad for the parents and what they were going through.

Both parents wept and we tried to comfort

Ben Carson

each other. "She was one of those children with such a fighting spirit," I heard myself telling the parents. "Why didn't she make it?" The pain hurt so deeply it seemed as if everybody in the world that I loved had died at one time. We never were able to discover why Jennifer died.

I share Jennifer's story because, despite our best efforts, not all our cases are successful. Some people cope with their failures more easily than others. I don't handle failure well. I've said to Candy several times, "I guess the Lord knows that, so he keeps it from happening to me often." In Jennifer's case, I could only keep going by reminding myself that there are a lot of other people out there who need help. It's unfair to them for me to dwell on the failures. But even now I'm not sure I have fully gotten over Jennifer's death.

12

Craig's Miracle

Twenty-five to thirty people had crowded into Craig Warnick's hospital room. They were holding a prayer meeting when I walked in. All of them were asking God for a miracle when Craig went into surgery. I stayed a few minutes and prayed too.

As I was leaving, Craig's wife, Susan, walked to the door with me. "Remember what your mother said," she told me with a warm smile. I had once quoted Mother's words to her: "If you ask the Lord for something, believing he will do it, then he will do it."

"And you remember it, too," I said. As I walked down the hall, I thought of all that Craig and Susan had been through. And it was nowhere near being over.

Susan is a nurse on our children's neurosurgical floor. Her husband has a rare disease called VHL (Von Hippel-Lindau disease). This disease causes many tumors to develop. Craig had gone through several serious operations over the past thirteen years that had left him crippled and unable to swallow. Each time he had fought back. Susan, Craig, and their families offered thanks to God for every sign of progress and prayed daily for more.

After years of therapy Craig was able to walk down the aisle in 1980 with a cane to marry Susan. But the tumors kept coming back. In September 1986, Susan realized he was showing symptoms of yet another brain tumor. She asked me to take Craig as a patient.

At that time I removed three tumors. A little while later, I went in to remove another tumor growing in the center of his brain. Each time Craig recovered, slowly but steadily. Then in 1988 came the dreaded news: Craig had developed another tumor. This one looked as though it might be in his brain stem, in an area that we probably could not reach without killing him. Only surgery would tell if that was indeed where the tumor was. Craig and Susan asked me to do the surgery. But there was no way I could fit him into my already overbooked schedule. I recommended that they see another surgeon at Johns Hopkins.

Before anything could be done, however,

Craig's condition worsened rapidly. He lost the ability to swallow and complained of severe headaches. On June 19, 1988, Craig was brought into the emergency room of the hospital. Susan called me. As I listened, I remembered all that Susan and Craig had gone through. I could not stand by and do nothing. I heard myself saying, "Okay, I'm going to bump somebody off the schedule. We'll get Craig into surgery."

Both Craig and Susan were overjoyed. I don't think I've ever seen two happier people. It seemed that just knowing I would do the surgery gave them a greater sense of peace.

"It's all in God's hands," I told them.

"But we believe you let God use your hands," Craig said.

I had to explain to Craig and Susan how serious this tumor was. "I can't tell for sure where it is until I go inside and see," I said. "But if it is inside the brain stem—" I paused, not wanting to tell them I wouldn't be able to do anything.

"We understand," Craig said. "It's going to be all right," Susan said. And she meant it. It felt strange having the patient's wife boosting my morale.

It was a tough operation. The tumor was surrounded by so many abnormal blood vessels that I had to use a microscope to even find where the tumor began. I looked up and down the brain

Ben Carson

stem but couldn't find anything. Then I knew that the tumor had to be inside that swollen brain stem.

After eight hours of surgery, we closed Craig up and sent him back to intensive care. The next morning I told Susan and Craig the bad news that the tumor was in the middle of a part of the brain stem called the pons.

"I'm willing to open the pons up," I said. "I couldn't risk doing it last night. I'd already been operating for eight hours and I was too tired. Even under the best conditions there is at least a fifty-fifty chance that Craig will die right on the table."

"Do it," said Craig.

"We understand," Susan said. "We want you to go ahead anyway. We are praying for a miracle. We believe God is going to do it through you."

I scheduled surgery for a few days later. Again it was tough going. As I started to open up the brain stem, it began to bleed heavily. Every time I touched the stem it bled. As my assistant suctioned up the blood, I asked myself, *What do I do now? God, help me know what to do.* I always pray before any operation, but this time I prayed during the entire surgery. *Lord, it's up to you. You've got to do something.*

At one point, I paused and stared into space. *Craig will die unless you show me what to do,* I prayed. Within seconds, I had a plan. "Let me have the laser," I said to a technician. Using the laser cautiously, I tried opening a small hole in the brain stem. The laser enabled me to seal off some of the bleeding vessels as I went. At last I got a tiny hole opened and went inside.

I felt something abnormal and tugged gently at it, but it was stuck. Again I hesitated, not wanting to take any chances. Because I was working in such a critical area, I did not dare open up the hole any larger. At that point I heard one of my surgical team members say, "The evoked potentials are gone." That meant that our instruments could no longer detect brain waves or activity on one side of Craig's brain. This was a sign of severe damage.

"We're in here. We're going to see it through," I said. I refused to let myself think about how severe the damage might be. *God,* I prayed, *I just can't give up. Please guide my hands.* I kept working at the tiny hole in the stem. I tugged, eased, and pulled at that cancerous blob, begging it to come out. Finally it started to pull loose. Gently I tugged again, and the tumor popped out in one gigantic blob.

But while I felt pleased that I had gotten the tumor, the damage to Craig had been done. Even if he did survive, which wasn't likely, he would be a "total train wreck." He would certainly be in a coma and probably paralyzed. When I finished the surgery four hours later, I felt terrible. Aloud I said, "Well, we did our best." I knew we had, but my words brought me no comfort.

When I met with Susan and the family in the waiting room, I had to tell them, "As I said before, this was likely to happen. At best, Craig will live a few more months and then die."

When I went to see Craig the next afternoon, I could not believe my eyes. He was sitting up in bed! I stared at him for several seconds. Then, to cover my amazement, I said, "Move your right arm."

He moved it.

"Now your left." Again, quite normal reactions. I asked him to move his feet and anything else I could think of. Everything was normal. I could not explain how he could be normal, but he was. Craig still had problems swallowing, but everything else seemed okay.

"I guess God had something to do with this," I said.

"I guess God had everything to do with this," he answered.

The next morning he was cracking jokes, having a fine time with the staff. "You got your miracle, Craig," I said.

"I know." His face glowed.

I was at home with my wife and my small boys one evening about six weeks later when the phone rang. It was Susan. Without bothering to identify herself, she shouted, "Dr. Carson! You won't believe what just happened! Craig ate a whole plate of spaghetti and meatballs! He ate it all. And he swallowed everything! That was more than half an hour ago, and he's feeling great."

We talked for some time. It felt good to know that I had been a part of Susan and Craig's lives during such a special moment. It felt good to have been part of a miracle.

13

Separating the Twins

This can't be true!" Theresa Binder cried. "I'm not having twins! I'm having a sick, ugly monster!" The twenty-year-old German mother had just been told that she would give birth to twins who were joined at the head.

She cried for three days. In her pain, she thought of overdosing on sleeping pills to kill the unborn twins and herself. She considered running away, jumping out of the window of a tall building. By the fourth morning, though, Theresa made peace with herself. She would face the tragedy and live with the results. Other parents had.

The twins, Patrick and Benjamin, were born on February 2, 1987. They were joined at the back of the head. When Theresa saw the babies for the first time three days later, her husband stood ready to catch her and carry her from the room if she fainted. Theresa stared at the infants. Words like monster fled from her. She saw only two tiny boys—her babies—and her heart melted. She and her husband hugged the boys. "You are ours," she said to the boys, "and I already love you."

Because they were joined at the heads, the boys could not learn to move like other infants. The Binders learned that if the boys remained attached, they would never sit, crawl, turn over, or walk. As they considered the limited future of Patrick and Benjamin, the Binders hoped for a miracle. The two boys shared a section of the skull as well as a major vein responsible for draining blood from the brain and returning it to the heart. No one had ever separated two such twins without at least one of the children dying. Other surgeons told Theresa Binder that it could not be done. One of the boys would have to be sacrificed in order for the other to live.

But Theresa Binder could not bear the thought of allowing one of her babies to die. She refused to give up hope. "I knew I would fight for their chance as long as I lived," she said.

Theresa Binder searched throughout the medical world. The Binders' doctors in Germany finally

Ben Carson

contacted us at Johns Hopkins. They wanted to know if we knew of any way to separate the twins so they could lead normal, separated lives.

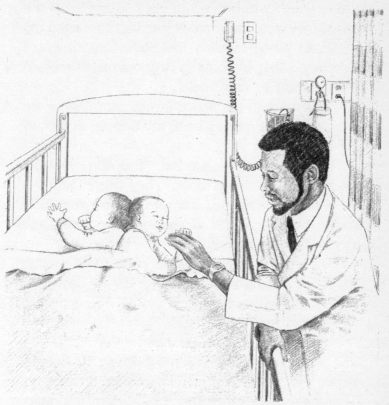

After studying the information, I agreed to consider what no other medical team in the world was willing to try. I knew that the kind of surgery we were planning would be the riskiest and most demanding I had ever done. But I also knew it would be the boys' only chance to live normally. Several of us made plans to fly to Germany in May 1987 to examine the twins. Then two weeks before I was to go, thieves broke into our house. One of the things they stole was a small safe that contained my passport. When I called the State Department, I discovered that it would be impossible to replace the passport in two weeks.

I then asked the police investigator, "What are the chances of getting back my papers, especially the passport?"

"No chance," he snorted. "You don't ever get those kinds of things back. They trash them."

After hanging up, I prayed, "Lord, somehow you've got to get me a passport if you want me involved in this surgery."

Two days later the same policeman phoned my office. "You won't believe this, but we have your papers. And your passport."

"Oh, I believe it," I said.

In an amazed tone, he told me that a detective had been going through some garbage. He found a paper with my name on it and kept on digging. Then he found all the other things, every important stolen document. Because of this, I was able to fly to Germany and meet the twins. While we were there, one of our team inserted inflatable balloons under the scalps of the babies. This device would gradually stretch the skin so that we would have enough skin to cover the huge wounds after separation.

The operation proved to be a gigantic undertaking. Counting all the surgeons, nurses, and technicians, there would be seventy of us involved in the surgery. All of us had to undergo five months of intensive study and training. We worked through every possible incident that could happen during surgery. We even worked out where each team member would stand on the operating room floor. A ten-page, play-by-play book detailed each step of the operation. We went through five, three-hour dress rehearsals using life-sized dolls attached at the head by Velcro.

Surgery on the seven-month-old twins began on September 5, 1987, at 7:15 A.M. We cut into the scalp and removed the bony tissue that held the two skulls. This we carefully preserved so that we could use it later to rebuild their skulls.

Next we opened the dura—a thin layer that covers the brain. This was no easy matter, especially since there was a large artery running between Patrick's and Benjamin's brains in that area. After this artery was sectioned off, we attempted to separate the venus sinuses. These are wide channels of blood in the outermost covering of the brain. These sinuses come together in a place called the torcula which is normally no larger than a half dollar.

But when we cut below the area where the torcula should have ended, we tapped into an alarming amount of blood. We proceeded even further down and ran into the same thing. "The torcula can't extend much further," I said. Yet I moved all the way down to the base of the skull and still found the same problem.

We were dismayed to find that the torcula covered the entire backs of the boys' heads. That meant that the twins had a gigantic, highly pressurized lake of blood back there. This unexpected situation forced us to change our plans. We had already made plans to stop the boys' blood flow long enough for us to construct separate veins. Now we had to get this process started sooner than we had intended.

Slowly we removed blood from the twins' bodies. Each child was hooked up to a heart-lung bypass machine. Their blood was pumped through this machine to cool their body temperatures down to 68 degrees Fahrenheit. This cooling brought their body functions to almost a complete halt. That would allow us to stop the heart and blood flow for about an hour without causing brain damage. This technique works only with infants whose undeveloped brains are flexible enough to recover from such a shock.

Twenty minutes after we started lowering the twins' body temperatures, the critical moment

Ben Carson

arrived. The blood flow was stopped. With the skulls already open, I cut the major vein that carried blood out of the brain. For the first time in their young lives, Patrick and Benjamin were living apart from each other.

We pulled the hinged table apart. Donlan Long had one boy, and I had the other. We were racing against the clock with two tiny lives at stake. Both Long and I had exactly one hour to fashion a new vein from the pieces of heart covering that we had removed earlier. I had already instructed the staff to turn the pumps back on when the hour was up. We could not take the chance of brain damage. "If they bleed to death then they'll have to bleed to death, but we'll know we did the best we could."

Someone started the big timer on the wall. "Please don't tell me what time it is or how much time we have left," I said to the nursing staff. I was working as fast as I could. I did not need the extra pressure of someone saying, "You've only got seventeen minutes left."

It was an eerie experience, starting the surgery. The baby's body was so cold it was like working on a corpse. In one sense, the twins were dead. Momentarily I wondered if they would ever live again.

14

"More Blood!"

In the planning sessions, I had allowed three to five minutes to cut through the sinuses. Then we would spend the remaining fifty to fifty-five minutes rebuilding the veins.

"Oh, no," I mumbled under my breath. I had already hit a snag. It would take me twenty minutes to separate all the vessels in the huge torcula area. I had to be extremely cautious because even a small hole in the torcula would cause a baby to bleed to death in less than a minute. That left only forty minutes to complete the rest of the job.

Other surgeons had been looking over our shoulders as I cut through the sinuses. They cut pieces to exactly the right diameter and shape that I

Ben Carson

needed for rebuilding. All of these pieces fit perfectly, and we were able to sew them into place. That saved us some time. Yet with about fifteen minutes to go, I knew we were moving close to the deadline. I could sense the anxiety around me.

Long completed his baby first. I finished mine just seconds before the blood started to flow again. Silence filled the room, except for the rhythmic humming of the heart-lung machine. "It's done," somebody said behind me.

I nodded, exhaling deeply, suddenly aware that I had been holding my breath during those last critical moments.

Once we restarted the infants' hearts, we hit our second big obstacle. Blood began pouring out of the many tiny blood vessels in the brain that had been severed during surgery. We had expected some bleeding because we had to thin their blood in order to use the heart-lung machine. This meant the blood would not be able to clot as it normally would. But now the bleeding was getting totally out of hand. Everything that could bleed did bleed.

For the next three hours, we tried everything known to the human mind to control the bleeding. Pint after pint of blood flowed through the twins' bodies. At one point we were certain they would not make it.

"More blood!" The silence of the operating room was smashed by that quiet command. By this time, the twins had received fifty units of blood, several dozen times more than their normal blood volume.

"There is no more blood," the reply came. "We've used it all." A quiet panic swept through the room. One of our team called the hospital blood bank.

"I'm sorry, but we don't have much blood on hand," said the voice on the other end of the line. "We've checked, and there is no more anywhere in the city of Baltimore."

As soon as we heard that, one of our team spoke up, "I'll give mine if you need it." Immediately six or eight other people in the operating room volunteered to donate blood. It was a noble gesture but not practical. Finally, the hospital blood bank called the American Red Cross. They came through with ten units—exactly the amount we needed.

While this was going on, someone from the team was staying in touch with the parents. We also had staff on hand to make sure those of us on the team had food to eat during our rare breaks.

Even when the bleeding was brought under control, there was no time to relax. The twins' brains had begun to swell dramatically. We had to work fast to get their scalps closed before their swelling brains came completely out of their skulls. We gave the boys a drug to put them into a coma to slow down the brain activity. Then Long and I stepped back as the plastic surgery team pieced the skull back together.

The surgery ended at 5:15 on Sunday morning. We had been working for twenty-two hours with only brief breaks to give the Binder twins their own separate lives. When our team came out of the operating room, we were met by applause from the other hospital staff members. One of our staff went directly to Theresa Binder. With a smile on his face, he asked, "Which child would you like to see first?"

She opened her mouth to respond, and tears filled her eyes. We all knew, though, that the battle was not over yet. The first step had been a giant one, and we had made it. But it was only the first step on a long road. In every phase of this surgery I had prayed silently, *Oh, God, let them live. Let them make it.* That prayer would be repeated many times in the next days.

Even with the successful surgery, I put the twins' chance of survival at no better than fifty-fifty. As pessimistic as I was about their future, I still felt a glow of pride in what we had accomplished. It seemed as if everyone from ward clerks to orderlies to nurses had become personally involved in this historic event. We were a team—a wonderful, marvelous team.

Patrick and Benjamin Binder remained in a coma for ten days. During that time we could do nothing but wait and wonder. Would they ever wake up? If so, could they live a normal life? Would they be handicapped? *It's all in God's hands,* I would say to myself. *That's where it's always been.*

For at least the next week, I could not relax at home. I just knew the phone would ring and I would hear the terrible news that the Binders had not made it. In the middle of the second week I stopped by to check on the twins. "They're moving," I said. "Look! He moved his left foot. See!"

"They're moving!" someone beside me said. "They're both going to make it!"

We were beside ourselves with joy, like new parents who must explore every inch of their new babies. Every movement from a yawn to the wiggling of toes became a cause for celebration throughout the hospital. Later that day came the moment that brought tears to many of us. Both boys opened their eyes and started looking around.

"He can see! They both can see!" someone cried.

"He's looking at me!" another person exclaimed.

We would have sounded crazy to anyone who did not know the long history of preparation, work, worry, and concern. We felt exhilarated. I had not expected the boys to survive for twenty-four hours, yet they were progressing nicely every day. "God, thank you, thank you," I said again and again. Theresa and Franz Binder returned to Germany later in 1989 with two separated and much-loved twin boys.

I know that God had a hand in this marvelous event, just as I know he has had a hand in shaping everything good in my life. Thanks to God and a courageous mother, a ghetto kid from the streets of Detroit has been able to take part in medical miracles. I have been blessed with a wonderful wife, three healthy boys, and a loving community of church friends.

I want God to use me to help others. I pray that I can be the best father and husband to my family, that I can be a caring member of my church and community. And I feel an obligation to act as a role model for young black people who feel trapped by their dismal situations. Perhaps I can't do much, but I can provide one living example of someone who came from a disadvantaged background and made it.

In May 1988 the *Detroit News* ran a feature story on me in their Sunday paper. After reading the article, a man wrote to me. He was a social worker and had a thirteen-year-old son who also wanted to be a social worker. However, things had not been going well. The father had been evicted from his apartment and then lost his job. He and his son were looking for their next meal, and his world had turned upside down. He was so depressed that he was ready to commit suicide. Then he picked up the *Detroit News* and read the article about me. He wrote:

"Your story just turned my life around and gave me hope. Your example inspired me to go on and put my best efforts into life again. I now have a new job, and things are starting to turn around. That article changed my life."

Letters like that let me know that, both in and out of the operating room, God's hand is still at work in my life.